TANTRA

First HarperCollins Edition 1995
Library of Congress number available on request

ISBN 0-06-251213-7

95 96 97 98 99 REED 10 9 8 7 6 5 4 3 2 1

WARNING: With the prevalence of AIDS and other sexually
transmitted diseases, if you do not practice safe sex you are
risking your life and your partner's life.

TANTRA

HarperSanFrancisco

A Division of HarperCollins*Publishers*

INTRODUCTION

Tantra is commonly believed to be centred around secret sexual rituals. Only a few *tantric* cults practise sacred sex, but it is probably true to say that nothing else comes so directly or closely to the heart of true *tantric* experience.

All *Tantras* are based on reverence for a dual male-female religious principle. In Hinduism this means the Great Mother goddess and her consort, usually Parvati-Kali and Shiva. The goddess and god are lovers, separate yet ultimately indistinguishable. When Shiva dances, it is Kali dancing within him. When Kali moves, it is Shiva moving within her limbs. In their lovemaking the god and goddess achieve a union that recalls their origin in a single, ineffable oneness which resides outside space and time.

The goal of the human *tantric* is to experience that state of primeval oneness. Or rather to re-experience it, since the human spirit is a true fragment of godhead that has become ensnared and entrapped in flesh. To the *tantric* all females are Kali. All males are Shiva. A couple may join together – if they know how – and by dissolving difference and separation, re-experience the primeval union. Of course this is not easily achieved. *Tantric* sex is a secret meditation, the object of which is to merge the two personalities and natures so completely that only one being is left breathing, seeing, thinking, laughing. As a form of meditation, the preparation for a sexual rite is no less rigorous than for any other kind of meditation. It involves a thorough theoretical and practical knowledge of *hatha yoga,* breath control, *mantra* (spells), yantra (sacred diagrams), *puja* (ritual) and kundalini yoga. *Tantric* sex is for adepts who have passed far beyond the beginners' techniques taught in the Kamasutram and other Hindu sex manuals.

The lover's body is a temple, to be worshipped. It is a sacred place, the home of the spirit. The *yoni* of the woman is a holy well, fount of life, source of miracles. The *lingam* of her partner is the creative power of the godhead itself. Each body is the whole world. To make love is to go on a pilgrimage and to arrive home.

As the writer of the *Kularnavatantra* says: '*Those who experience the bliss of merging their souls into the One – they know the meaning of sexual union. All the others just copulate.*'

VAMAKESVARATANTRAM

*If you must learn about sexual love, learn from an
expert and learn that it is founded in compassion.
O Goddess, the fully awakened adept may
worship with honey, syrup, milk, wheat, perfumes,
flowers, fine clothes and jewels – but when he
worships with sexual union, he worships with
woman, who is the image of the Mother of the
Universe.*

(before 1750 AD)

MAHANIRVANATANTRAM

Again, it is you, O God, who has revealed in a thousand different forms, the rites of worship with a woman – woman, who embraces man like a creeper clinging to a tree – and also the kinds of women with whom worship may be conducted in a tantric rite.

(19th century AD)

आदिवृद्धशयनभितकृ तणाहियु पुरीरस नेकि विविसो मु कुळुई खतकृ वरुखया
पाल स्तितिय पुरुषोवृ यते मुळ विसि

SONG OF RAMAPRASADA

Who is this dark beauty coming this way?
Who can she be, young and lovely,
Naked yet devoid of shame, charming
everyone she meets?
See how she walks, loose-hipped –
How unseemly for such a respectable lady.
She's clearly been at the wine,
Laughing and lolling her tongue at us,
Her hair floating loose about her.
Just the sight of Her makes men and Gods tremble.

(12th century AD)

MANTRAMAHODADHI

While meditating upon the yoni of a beautiful woman, the adept shall utter the sacred mantra ten thousand times. He shall become as wise as Brhaspati. Ten thousand times more shall he repeat it, whilst meditating upon the yoni of a woman in her moon-time and he shall become as captivating as any practioner of the poetic art. At night he shall join his body together with a woman's and repeat the magic syllables one hundred thousand times. After this, he becomes like a king.

(1589 AD)

Mantramahodadhi

Up to this moment, whatever was thought, said or done by my mind, tongue, hands, feet and penis, whether in a waking, dreaming or sleeping state, whether pertinent to the spirit, the mind, or the body – I dedicate it utterly and completely to the absolute One.

(1589 AD)

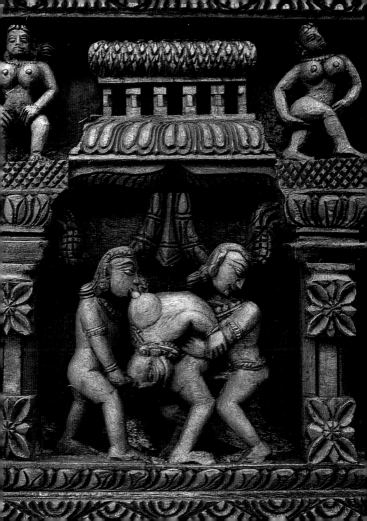

SIVASAMHITA

*Where is kundalini to be found? In that region
between the anus and the spring of water is the
yoni, the organ of creation, its mouth opened
towards the earth. Around this cave are twined the
roots of kundali. Here she can always be found,
coiled three and a half times around the body's
vital nerves with her tail in her mouth.*

(1st century AD)

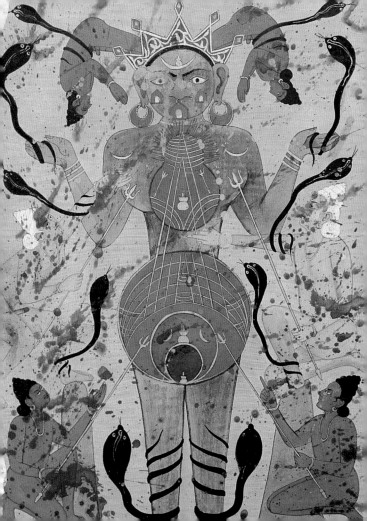

MAHANIRVANATANTRAM

The tantric and his wife should meditate together, seated side by side on their bed. Let him place his left arm about her shoulders and with his right hand invoke the goddess into her body, uttering the appropriate mantras as he touches and blesses her head, her chin, her throat and each of her two breasts. Let him recite the mantra ten times over her heart and twenty five times over her navel.

*Touching her vulva, let him recite the magic
formula one hundred and eight times and again
one hundred and eight times over his own penis.
Now let him open her vulva and, uttering the
magical syllable 'hrirn', enter. To get a child, at the
instant his seed flows he must be rapt in Brahma.*

(19th century AD)

KAULAVALITANTRAM

On the left a woman skilled in the sexual art. On the right a drinking cup. Between them a dish of spiced pork. On her shoulder a melodious lute with which to proclaim all the virtues; thus the most excellent Kaula faith, deep and mysterious to understand.

(10th century AD)

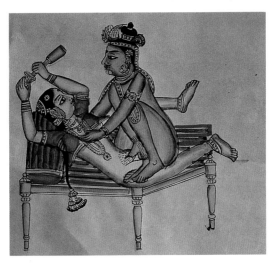

BRHADARANYAKOPANISAD

*Woman, in truth, is the fire of sacrifice, O
Gautama. Her lower limbs are the fuel, the hairs
of her body the smoke and her vulva itself the
flame. The act of entry is the kindling, the blaze of
pleasure is the sparks flying up; in this fire the gods
offer the seed of man, and from this offering man
is born. So long as he is destined to live, he lives.
And then dies.*

(circa 8th century AD)

KAULAJNANANIRNAYA

The goddess merges with Siva, her lover, who is found at the heart of every virtuous action, which action leads indissolubly to knowledge, knowledge endlessly becoming desire by virtue of which the goddess merges with Siva, her lover ...

(10th century AD)

When the woman brings her feet together and the man's thighs grip her waist, it is Kauliraka: the lovemaking of the Kaula tantrics. If during the lovemaking of the Kaulas, the man causes his partner to sway back and forth, why this is known to the tantrics as Prenkhi (the Swing) and is said to be a route to perfect peace.

(circa 17th century AD)

KAMASUTRAM

Every woman should know the joy of orgasm.
Every man should learn the arts of love and
should seek his partner's pleasure before his own.
Since there is no such thing as an ideal couple, it
would be unintelligent to lay down rules for love-
making. Only experience can tell what gives most
pleasure to whom. The wise are also aware that
physical pleasure is not the sole end of sexual
union. For people of intelligence and sensitivity, no
further explanation is needed.

(circa 4th century AD)

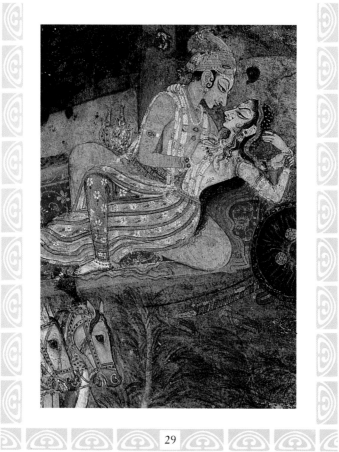

SRNGARARASAPRABANDHADIPIKA
With her limbs entwined in his, kissing and
playing a hundred sweet love games, the darling
girl usurps his rightful role. This is called Valli
(The Creeper). When they lie sprawled, clasping
one another's hands, her breasts stabbing his chest,
his thighs caressing hers, it is known as
Devabandha, the Lovemaking of the Gods.

(medieval)

BABHRAVYAKARIKA

Sayeth Auddalaki: 'In knowing man the lust of blissful women does abate, yet no kisse, love-drurye, or thruste of phallos does her passion sate, but knowledge of her heart-mate. Yet in spending is his pleasure's end, whilst her fierce ardour knows no cease, for in love's battle both must spend and blend their seed ere she finds peace.'

(1st millenium BC)

KAMASUTRAM

The old texts on lovemaking have mostly been lost. The fragments that survive are obscure, their language too old-fashioned for our modern taste. Feeling that this important subject deserves a contemporary treatment, I, Mallanaga Vatsyayana, have composed this slender Kamasutram, a summary of all that is known about love.

(circa 4th century AD)

Laksmidara's Commentary on
Saundaryalahari

*The eastern Kaulas in their sacred circles perform
the 'nine-yoni' ritual, establishing a living yoni in
their midst and worshipping with perfumes, gold
and clothes. The northern Kaulas in their medita-
tions do no more than visualise the yoni of a
young woman. Both forms of yoni worship, the
metaphorical and the literal, may be practised for
the fulfilment of desires. One's own wife, duly
adorned, consecrated and made lovely, can be both
goddess and paramour in this more-than-mortal
way of loving.*

(12th century AD)

YONITANTRAM

*The devotee who at prayers utters the sacred cry
'yoni, yoni', is blessed by the goddess and enjoys
both pleasure and freedom. The rites of yoni-
worship may be practised with an actress, a
beggarwoman, prostitute, laundress, brahmin
woman, or the daughters of barbers, labourers,
cowherds or garlandmakers. But one should
worship only the yoni of a mature woman, never a
virgin as doing this latter dissipates one's magical
powers.*

(probably 16th century)

RITUSAMHARA

She likes to watch her lover enjoy her body, her blouse opened up to him, her limbs aching, scored by his fingernails; a shy smile creeps to her mouth and curls of soft black hair come loose and fall down to cover her eyes.

(5th century AD)

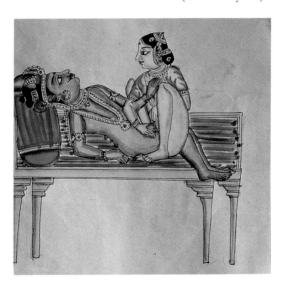

RITUSAMHARA

Other lovely and charming young women are also
feeling the dull heaviness of limbs which, slim and
well turned, would much rather be making love.
And when the masseuse works on them, her
fingers releasing the tension in the shoulders,
pressing the deep fold of the thighs, their nipples
start up, thrilling to the intimate touch.

(5th century AD)

Brhadaranyakopanisad

He was alone and felt no happiness. (Who feels happy when they are alone?) In his longing for another, he grew bigger, big as a man and a woman joined in lovemaking. He separated this body and divided it in two. The two parts were husband and wife. Indeed, says sage Yajnavalkya, this body is like half of a double-celled seed. Within each human is a void that can be filled only by one's other half. The two unite and thus are humans born.

(circa 8th century BC)

DEVIMAHATMYA

There, O King, in the high home of ice, dwells a woman so lovely that her beauty lights the snowy peaks. So perfect a body, such flawless limbs, have never before been seen in this world. Find out who she is and kidnap her, O demon Lord. (Little did this demon know that the lovely woman he would try to seize was none other than the great Goddess.)

(4th century AD)

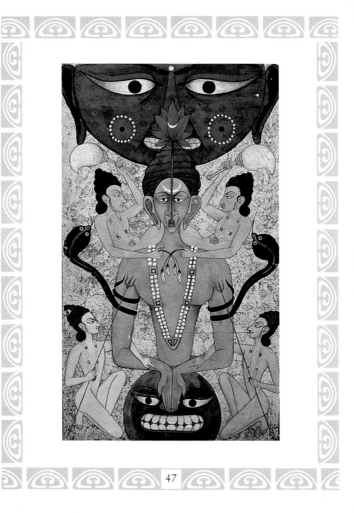

PRASNOPANISAD

Day and night are truly the masters of the world. Day is the abode of the spirit, and night the realm of the senses. Those who join their bodies during the day spill not just their seed but their very life. Those who pursue their loveplay in the time of stars know the true meaning of chastity.

(circa 8th century BC)

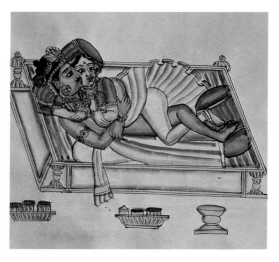

KATHOPANISAD

*People of small vision pursue sensual pleasures and
walk into the trap that death has set, for the wise
do not seek the eternal among perishable things.
But who is it that enjoys the sights, tastes, smells,
sounds and touches of love – who feels? Who is it
that knows? This, truly, is the point.*

(8th century BC)

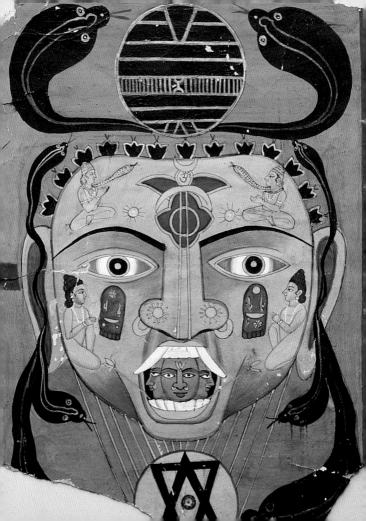

Bliss, you know, has the shape of a person. It can even look like you. Pleasure is its head, delight is its right side, even greater delight is its left side, sheer joy forms its body and at its root there is God.

(circa 8th century BC)

AITAREYOPANISAD

Fire becomes speech and flares from the mouth.
Air becomes breath and streams through the
nostrils. The sun becomes sight and shines in the
skull. Dark space becomes hearing and harkens at
the ears. Trees become hairs that root themselves
in the skin. The moon becomes a mind that shines
out from the heart. Death becomes an exhalation,
perched in the navel. Water becomes semen and
waits to be born.

(circa 8th century BC)

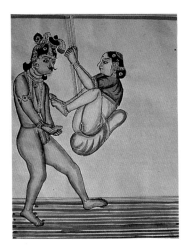

CHANDOGYOPANISAD

Then said Prajapati to the pair of them, 'put on your best clothes and your jewels, make yourselves look nice, then look into this bowl of water.' So the two of them put on their best clothes, wore their jewels and made themselves look good, then they looked into the water bowl. 'Now,' said Prajapati, 'what do you see?'

(circa 8th century BC)

*He parts her thighs, saying, 'Spread apart, heaven
and earth'. Then, sliding his phallus into her womb
and joining his mouth to hers, he strokes the hairs
about her yoni thrice and cries out 'Visnu prepare
this womb'. So she will conceive.*

(circa 8th century BC)

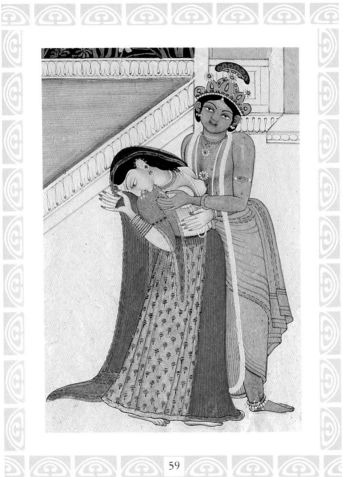

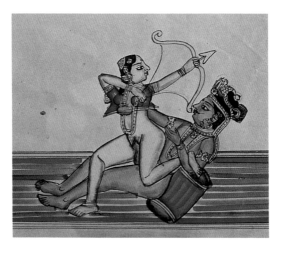

BRHADARANYAKOPANISAD

If one wishes a woman to enjoy lovemaking one should, after introducing the phallus, kissing her mouth and stroking her yoni, recite: 'You who dwell in every limb, who spring from the heart, whose spirit suffuses this body, help me astonish this woman, let her feel that she is pierced by an amazing arrow'.

(circa 8th century BC)

ATHARVAVEDA

O man, if you have controlled lust, anger, greed, desire, pride and ego; if you have mastered the senses, thought and intellect; if you know the eight branches of yoga; if you fully understand your body with its nine gates; then your pleasure will know no bounds. If not, you are powerless.

(2nd millenium BC)

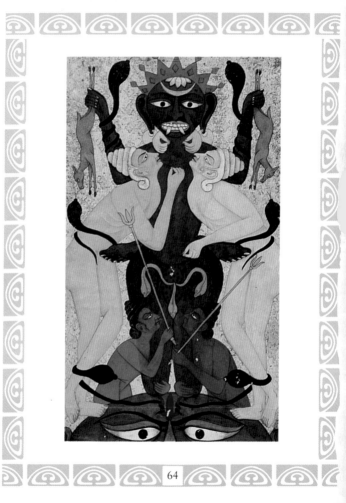